Augustine of Hippo

by Simonetta Carr

with Illustrations by Wes Lowe

REFORMATION HERITAGE BOOKS

Grand Rapids, Michigan

Augustine of Hippo
© 2009 by Simonetta Carr

Cover artwork by Wes Lowe: Augustine's Conversion. For additional artwork by Wes, see pages 10, 15, 18, 20, 26, 30, 34, 36, 38, 43, 45, 54.

All rights reserved. No part of this book may be used or reproduced in any manner whatsoever without written permission except in the case of brief quotations embodied in critical articles and reviews. Direct your requests to the publisher at the following address:

Reformation Heritage Books
2965 Leonard St. NE
Grand Rapids, MI 49525
616-977-0889 / Fax: 616-285-3246
e-mail: orders@heritagebooks.org
website: www.heritagebooks.org

Library of Congress Cataloging-in-Publication Data

Carr, Simonetta.
  Augustine of Hippo / by Simonetta Carr ; with illustrations by Wes Lowe.
    p. cm. — (Christian biographies for young readers)
  ISBN 978-1-60178-073-7 (hardcover : alk. paper) 1. Augustine, Saint, Bishop of Hippo—Juvenile literature. 2. Christian saints—Algeria—Hippo (Extinct city)—Biography—Juvenile literature. I. Lowe, Wesley. II. Title.
  BR1720.A9C28 2009
  270.2092—dc22
  [B]
                                        2009041833

For additional Reformed literature, request a free book list from Reformation Heritage Books at the above address.

Printed in the United States of America
12 13 14 15 16 17/10 9 8 7 6 5 4 3 2

CHRISTIAN BIOGRAPHIES FOR YOUNG READERS

This series introduces children to important people in the Christian tradition. Parents and schoolteachers alike will welcome the excellent educational value it provides for students, while the quality of the publication and the artwork make each volume a keepsake for generations to come. Furthermore, the books in the series go beyond the simple story of someone's life by teaching young readers the historical and theological relevance of each character.

AVAILABLE VOLUMES OF THE SERIES
John Calvin
Augustine of Hippo
John Owen
Athanasius
Lady Jane Grey

SOME ANTICIPATED VOLUMES
Anselm
John Knox
Jonathan Edwards
…and more

Acknowledgments

I give a heartfelt thank-you to all the people who have reviewed this book: my children Christian, Simon, Dustin, David, Jonathan, Kevin, Raphael, and Renaissance; Prof. Phillip Cary, Professor of Philosophy at Eastern University in St. Davids, Pennsylvania; Dr. Scott Clark, Professor of Church History and Historical Theology at Westminster Seminary California; Dr. Richard Bishop, Historical Theology, University of Virginia; Travis Baker, doctoral student of Medieval History at Oxford University; and Rev. Michael Matossian, Pastor of Emmanuel Orthodox Presbyterian Church, Wilnoughton, Delaware. I want to thank those who have sent photos of places or works of art, particularly Dr. Luigi Beretta of Centro Culturale Agostiniano, historian James J. O'Donnell, poet Karl Lubomirski, and Teresa Roth of Heritage History.

As well, I offer a special thank-you to the Reformation Heritage Books staff, particularly Jay Collier and Steve Renkema, for their patience and support; to my friend Dianna Ippolito of Besame Photography for her artistic advice and for providing some photos to the illustrator; and to my husband, Tom, my mother, Luciana, my friend Kris Moberly, and all my church family (especially Rev. Michael Brown and Rev. Dr. Michael Horton), for their constant encouragement.

Table of Contents

Introduction 7

Chapter 1: Growing Up 8

Chapter 2: In Search of Wisdom 13

Chapter 3: Italy 21

Chapter 4: A Decision to Follow God 29

Chapter 5: A Minister against His Will 33

Chapter 6: Difficult Times 42

Chapter 7: Augustine's Last Days 52

Time Line 57

Did You Know? 59

As you read this book, you can follow Augustine's travels on this map.

Introduction

During Augustine's life, the Roman Empire ruled most of what are now Europe and the Middle East. It was divided into two parts: the Western Roman Empire (with Milan as its capital) and the Eastern Roman Empire (with Constantinople as its capital). Augustine lived in the Western Roman Empire.

Augustine was born on November 13, 354 A.D. His full name was Aurelius Augustinus. We call him Augustine of Hippo because he spent most of his life in the city of Hippo Regius, in North Africa. He is still considered one of the greatest thinkers who ever lived. Even people who are not Christians admire the way in which he explained things that cannot be seen and touched, like faith, God's grace, and love.

Augustine

No one knows what Augustine looked like. The earliest portrait that we still have today was done about two hundred years after his death. As you see in this book, artists imagined Augustine in their own special way.

CHAPTER ONE
Growing Up

Augustine's birthplace was a small town in Northern Africa named Thagaste. Today, the whole region around Thagaste is called Algeria. It was a very green area, full of farms, and olive and wheat fields. Augustine grew up like many children in the Roman Empire. The books he studied were mostly written in Latin, which was the language spoken in ancient Rome.

Fields in Algeria, similar to those Augustine would have seen as a child

The emperor Constantine

After Jesus' resurrection, Christians were often persecuted and killed by the Roman government. All that changed about forty years before Augustine's birth, when Emperor Constantine made Christianity a legal religion. Then, Christians actually received so many privileges that other people did not have, that many said they were Christians even if they really did not believe. Augustine's father, Patricius, did not believe in Jesus, but his mother, Monica, did, and taught her children to do the same.

Augustine studied in Thagaste and in a nearby city until the age of sixteen. Because he was very smart, his father decided to send him to Carthage, the largest city in that region, to study law and the art of giving speeches.

Augustine stole pears from a neighbor.

Speaking well in public was a very respected skill in those days. Anyone who wanted to have an important job in society as a politician, teacher, lawyer, or church leader, had to learn how to speak clearly and to convince others that what he said was true. Patricius knew that if his son could speak well he could make a good career in this world. Being a small government officer in Thagaste, Patricius did not have enough money to send his son to Carthage right away, so Augustine had to spend about a year at home.

As a teenager with nothing better to do, Augustine spent a lot of time with a group of naughty friends, looking for fun and playing all kinds of pranks. One night, they went into a neighbor's field and stole a bunch of pears from his tree. They ate a few and, since they really did not care about the pears, gave the rest to the pigs. Later, Augustine looked back at this time of his life. He was surprised as he realized that he had stolen those pears just for the pleasure of stealing. This showed him how much we all, left to ourselves, tend to sin.

Some ruins of ancient Carthage

CHAPTER TWO

In Search of Wisdom

Finally, a friend of Augustine's father helped the young teenager move to Carthage to continue his studies. Carthage was busy, full of life, and very different from the small town of Thagaste. Many students, caught in the excitement of the big city, were rowdy and unruly.

Augustine had many friends, even if he did not like everything they did. He was a very good student and an excellent speaker. As a student, he read many books written by a famous Roman speaker named Cicero. One of Cicero's books in particular gave him a great desire to know the true meaning of wisdom.

Cicero

Augustine had been raised as a Christian, but did not know the Bible well. The Latin translation of the Bible at that time was not very good, and Augustine found it different from the fancy, well-written textbooks he used to study. He also did not understand many of the Old Testament stories, which he found hard to believe. Disappointed, he put the Bible aside.

At that same time, he found a group of people who called themselves Manichees. They claimed to be Christians, but taught many things which are not in the Bible. Augustine liked them because they spoke very well.

Monica, Augustine's mother, was very sad about her son's choice, and prayed every day that he would have faith in the true God. Once she had a dream where she was standing on a big wooden ruler, crying, and a young man told her not to worry, because Augustine was standing on the same ruler too. "He will be where you are," the young man said.

Monica's dream

Encouraged, Monica told her son that the dream meant that he would become a Christian like her. Augustine was not sure. "Maybe you will become a Manichee like me!" Monica stood her ground. "The man in my dream said that you will be where I am, not that I will be where you are," she explained. Augustine was impressed by those words more than by the dream itself. This great speaker, able to win the toughest debates, was now silenced by his mother's wisdom and conviction. For many years, he thought carefully about Monica's reply.

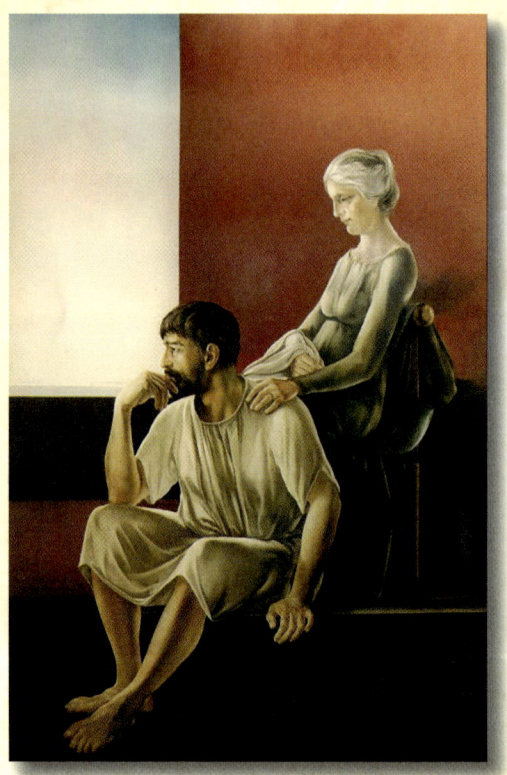

Augustine and his mother Monica

Painting by Ezio Pollai, Chiesa dell' Eremo, Lecceto (SI), Italy

Without losing hope, Monica kept praying and crying to God for her son. Once she talked to a priest who had also been a Manichee. "Augustine will eventually find out how wrong they are," he told her. Because Monica kept crying and asking him to talk to her son, he added, "The son of a mother who sheds so many tears for him cannot perish."

As soon as Augustine finished his studies, he went back to Thagaste to teach others how to give good speeches. He had many friends who shared his beliefs and liked to do the same things. One day, his very best friend got very sick with a high fever and became unconscious. It seemed that he was going to die, so his family baptized him, hoping that it could make some difference.

Surprisingly, his friend got better. When he opened his eyes, Augustine told him what happened, "When you were unconscious, they baptized you!" He thought it was very funny, because his friend was a Manichee, and Manichees made fun of the church and the sacraments.

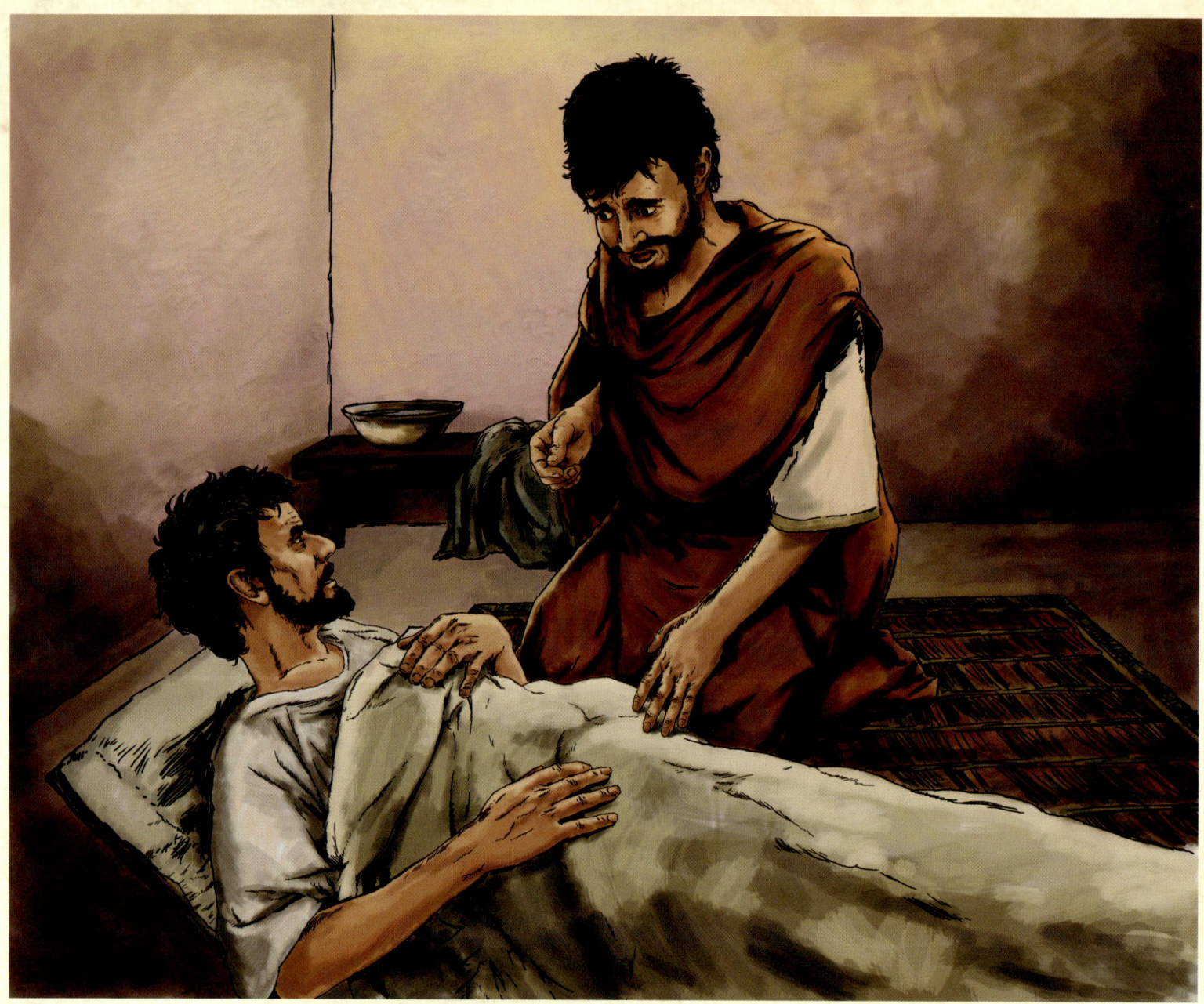

Augustine's friend told Augustine to stop teaching him all that Manichean nonsense.

He expected his friend to laugh or to get angry with those who had baptized him. Instead, his friend got angry with Augustine and told him that if he wanted to stay his friend, he would have to stop teaching him all that Manichean nonsense. Augustine was shocked. He had always thought that baptism was just an empty ceremony. Looking back at this experience many years later, he realized that baptism is instead God's mark of His work in our souls.

Augustine waited a while. He thought that his friend would start following the Manichees again, but his friend got sick again and died. This plunged Augustine into deep sorrow. Losing such a close friend meant losing an important part of his life. He could not find any joy because everything reminded him of his friend. "I hated all places because he was not in them, because they could not say to me, 'Look, he is coming,'" Augustine wrote.

Augustine left for Italy while his mother was praying.

CHAPTER THREE
Italy

To get away from his sad memories, Augustine returned to Carthage where he became a respected and well-known teacher. His students, however, were very unruly, so he became frustrated. Some friends told him that he could have a better career in Rome, where students were more polite. Augustine decided to take their advice. His father, who had finally become a Christian, had already died, so Monica wanted to go with Augustine. However, Augustine did not want to take his mother along. He told her to wait for him inside a little church by the port, while he stayed with a friend who was waiting for favorable winds to sail. But there was no friend waiting. It was just a cruel lie. While his mother was praying, Augustine left for Rome, leaving her behind.

The Roman Forum, an important part of the city where people gathered for justice and for discussions, as it looks today. Augustine probably taught and spoke there.

In Rome, Augustine was not happy. He felt uneasy about leaving his mother and was disappointed by his students, who were lazy and did not pay their bills. His biggest disappointment was with the Manichees, who were also popular in Rome. He started to see that their teachings were wrong, but he still did not know what was right. Finally, some friends introduced him to a person who had been trying for some time to find a good professor for the Emperor's court in Milan, in the north of Italy.

The Roman Forum as it probably looked in Ancient Rome

Augustine was chosen for this position, one of the most important teaching jobs in the whole Roman Empire. He was about thirty years old. In Milan, he met the man in charge of all the churches in that area. His name was Ambrose. People in charge of many churches were called bishops. Bishop Ambrose was older and more experienced than Augustine was and, like him, knew how to speak well and clearly. His sermons answered many of Augustine's questions about God and the Bible.

Ambrose of Milan

Ruins of the ancient Roman Imperial Palace in Milan

Around that time, Monica arrived in Milan. She was very happy to see Augustine settled with a good job, and she really admired Ambrose. She thought Ambrose could help her son to become a true Christian. However, becoming a Christian was not easy for Augustine. He felt that there were two wills inside of him—one wanted to know God and live for Him and the other did not. One part of him wanted to study the Scriptures and know the truth, and the other part only wanted to have a good career, money, fame, and material joys. He tried to postpone the decision. "Give me just a little while longer," he would ask God. But as he wrote later, "just a little while went on for a long while."

Augustine sees a beggar.

One day Augustine was walking down a street in Milan with some friends. His head was full of thoughts and worries as he got ready to give an important speech before the Emperor himself. He knew that his speech was going to be full of lies but that was what everyone expected him to say. Suddenly, he saw a beggar who, in spite of his poverty, seemed happy because he had no cares and was not trying to impress anyone. Augustine thought for a while. If the goal of his life was to find happiness, this beggar had found it in a much quicker and easier way. He understood then the emptiness of his search for money and fame.

One day Augustine visited an old man named Simplicianus, who was well known and respected for his faith in God. Simplicianus told Augustine some stories of other young people who had been faced with the same difficult decisions.

One of Simplicianus's stories was about a famous young speaker named Victorinus who called himself a Christian and wanted to become a part of God's church, but did not think he needed to be baptized. Every time he said he was a Christian, Simplicianus would tell him, "I will not believe it until I see you in the church of God." To that, the young man always replied, "Do walls make a Christian?" Finally, the Scriptures convinced this man that it was important to profess his faith before the church and to be baptized.

Simplicianus

It was an important step for Victorinus. In those days famous people were not required to profess their faith in public, which could put them in danger. Victorinus's public baptism showed his courage and faithfulness to the truth. This and other stories heard from Simplicianus and from some of his friends showed Augustine that he needed to make a similar surrender.

CHAPTER FOUR
A Decision to Follow God

One day, as Augustine was lying down under a tree in a garden, praying to God in tears to help him end his terrible indecision, he heard a little child sing, "Take up and read! Take up and read!" It was probably a little children's song, but Augustine took it as an invitation to take up his Bible and read it. The first words that he read were Romans 13:13–14, which told him to put on the Lord Jesus Christ as a new robe, and to stop giving in to his sinful nature. The Holy Spirit used this experience to bring Augustine to a true conversion.

Now Augustine was no longer undecided. He really wanted to be a Christian. He told his friends and his mother, who rejoiced with him. Later, looking back at all the struggle he had faced before the Holy Spirit converted him and at the peace he felt afterward, he said, "Thou hast made us for Thyself, O Lord, and our heart is restless until it rests in Thee."

Augustine in the garden

Around that time, Augustine became ill. A pain in his chest made it impossible for him to continue his work as a teacher and speaker. A friend from Africa let him stay at his big villa near Milan, where Augustine was free to study and write. Augustine accepted the offer gladly, taking along his mother and other friends who had also become Christians. Together, they studied and discussed the Bible, excited about the truth that they were discovering. After about six months, Augustine returned to Milan with two of his friends and studied under Ambrose until they were ready to publicly profess their faith and be baptized. Augustine was then thirty-three years old.

Ruins of a Roman Villa in Carthage

The following year, Augustine decided to leave Milan to return to Africa with his mother and some friends. They planned to live together in Thagaste, just as they had done in the villa near Milan. Because of some fighting in Rome, they had to stop in Ostia, a small town near the Italian coast. There, Monica became very ill and died. Until that time, she had always wanted to be buried next to her husband, but now she did not care anymore. She was just happy that her son was finally a true Christian. Losing his mother was a very sad experience for Augustine, who mourned her death for many days.

Finally, around the end of 388, Augustine and his friends were able to leave Italy and return to North Africa, where they continued to live together, studying, discussing their discoveries, and writing.

Roman ruins at Ostia

CHAPTER FIVE
A Minister against His Will

The believers in Africa liked Augustine very much because of his writings, especially those where Augustine explained clearly why the teachings of the Manichees were not in the Scriptures. One day, as Augustine attended church in a town named Hippo, where he was visiting some friends, Valerius, the bishop who was preaching, noticed him in the crowd and announced that the church needed young, intelligent people who could stop false teachers like the Manichees. Everyone knew that he was talking about Augustine.

Remains of Augustine's church in Hippo Regius

PHOTO BY JAMES J. O'DOLLEY, PRIVATE COLLECTION

The people push Augustine forward to become priest.

Immediately, the people in church surrounded Augustine and pushed him forward, where the bishop ordained him as a minister of the gospel, or priest, right there on the spot. This was not strange in those days, but it would be now. Augustine started to cry. The people thought that he was crying because he was going to be only a priest, when he deserved to be a bishop. "Don't worry," they told him. "You will be a bishop very soon." However, Augustine was crying because he thought of all the hardships and dangers of that position and did not know if he had the strength to face them.

Augustine started his work in the church by teaching catechism. Everyone was impressed by his lessons because they were very clear. Soon he called his friends to join him in Hippo and found a place where they could live together. Their home was always so full of guests that they had to build a separate building to host them all. Augustine and his friends were always giving to the poor, keeping just the bare necessities for themselves.

Augustine debates with Fortunatus.

At that time, there was in Hippo a famous Manichee named Fortunatus. The Christians knew that Fortunatus's teachings were wrong, but they had never been able to clearly understand why, much less to prove it. They knew that Augustine was very smart and could speak very well, so they organized a debate where Augustine and Fortunatus would meet and discuss their different views in front of an audience. The debate lasted two days. In those days, debates were held in public squares, with great crowds listening. Augustine asked Fortunatus some difficult questions about his teachings. Not being able to answer, Fortunatus said that he wanted to go back and discuss them with his leaders. After that, he never came back to Hippo. Augustine had obviously won the debate.

AUGUSTINE OF HIPPO

A bishop gives a Bible to a Roman soldier.

The other group of people who gave problems to the church at Hippo was the Donatists, who believed that they were the only pure church in the world. About one hundred years before, when Christians were being persecuted, the Roman Empire had forced many bishops to give them their Bibles. The Donatists thought that those bishops should have never given their books to their enemies, and called them traitors. Then, because those bishops appointed the next priests and bishops, they thought that all the leaders of the church were corrupted.

"We need to start again," they said, "with a new church free of corruption." Augustine and Valerius knew that no church will ever be perfect in this world, so they worked together to explain to the Donatists that Christians should be united, and not divide every time someone makes a mistake. The Donatists had written many songs about their beliefs, so Augustine made up an ABC song in reply, starting each line with a different letter of the alphabet.

Augustine debating the Donatists
Painting by Carle Van Loo

Valerius and Augustine made a good team. They were energetic, passionate, and not afraid to try new things. In Africa, only the bishops were allowed to preach. Valerius, however, knew that those rules were not unbreakable and allowed Augustine to preach only two years after becoming a priest. He was so sure that Augustine was needed in Hippo that once he even hid him when some people arrived from another city, because he was afraid that they might take Augustine and make him their bishop!

Augustine preaching in front of Valerius

Painting by Carle Van Loo

Because Valerius was getting old, he needed someone to take his place. At a meeting of bishops, he proposed that Augustine take his position. Now that Augustine had proved his value, everyone gladly accepted this proposal. Augustine was not sure. Usually, a priest could take the place of a bishop only after the bishop's death, and Augustine did not want to be an exception. However, the bishops convinced him that he was not the first case, so he finally agreed. As a bishop, Augustine preached thousands of sermons. His friends wrote many of them down and we can still read them today.

The most ancient portrait of Augustine available today

CHAPTER SIX
Difficult Times

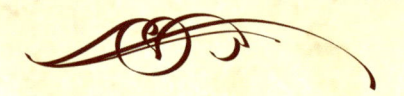

In those days, a Christian bishop could help people solve arguments just like a judge. Because it was easier to talk to a bishop than to a judge, many people came to Augustine every day, often from early morning until late afternoon. Augustine disliked this task the most, because he had to spend all day with loud, demanding people who wanted a solution to their problems, but continued to argue after leaving him.

After a full day of exhausting work, Augustine was glad to return to his friends who gave him counsel and encouragement. After a while, however, his friends were called to become bishops in other cities. Their departure was very painful for Augustine. Whenever he could, he traveled to visit them.

Augustine working as a judge

DIFFICULT TIMES

43

Augustine had many enemies too, especially among the Manichees and the Donatists, who were angry because he won every debate. One group of Donatists was particularly violent. Thinking they were purifying the church, some of them went around with clubs, beating and even killing other Christians. They were called Circumcellions. Augustine traveled often to visit other believers or to meet with other church leaders. One day, a group of Circumcellions discovered that Augustine was about to travel to a nearby town and they laid an ambush to try to kill him. Without knowing this, Augustine, in God's kind providence, went a different way and arrived safely at his destination.

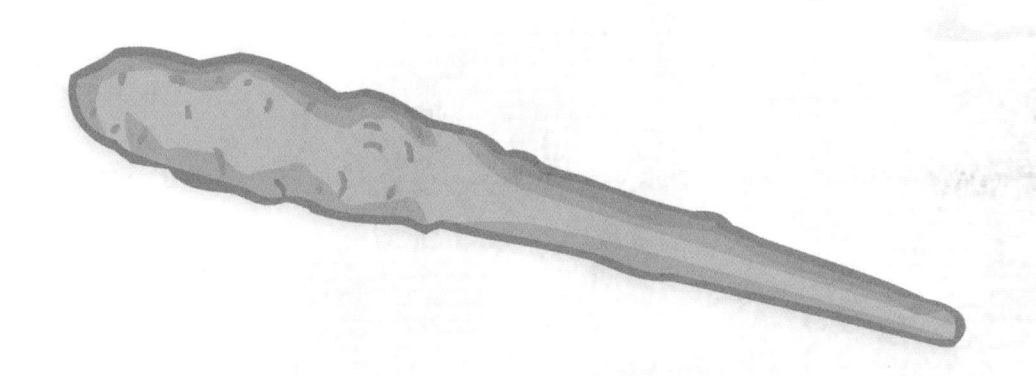

The Circumcellions try to attack Augustine.

DIFFICULT TIMES

At the age of forty-three, Augustine wrote a very famous book about his life, from the time he was a baby until his decision to serve God. It is called *Confessions*. It is really a long prayer to God, where Augustine remembered the events of his life and the lessons learned. Looking back at his younger years, he realized how deeply he had sinned against his mother, against his friends, and especially against God. He felt very sorry and ashamed, but also grateful to God for His forgiveness.

Readers are usually impressed by Augustine's honesty and ability to describe his emotions. He thought that it was important for people to understand their feelings and their beliefs, and be able to see what caused them to choose certain things.

In his *Confessions*, Augustine also recognized God's hand in his life. Everything that had happened had been used by God to make him the man God wanted him to be. For example, when Augustine lied to his mother to try to escape her and her religion, he didn't know that he was fulfilling God's plan of bringing him to Italy where he was converted and baptized.

Augustine as seen by Vittore Carpaccio, an artist from the Italian Renaissance

For this, Augustine was very thankful. But he was also sorry that it had taken him so long to love God. "Late have I loved Thee, O Beauty so ancient and so new! Late have I loved Thee! Thou wast within me and I was outside," he said, meaning that God had been speaking to his heart for a long time but he had been too busy with other things. You can ask your parents to read some parts of this beautiful book to you.

In 410, the Visigoths, an Eastern European tribe, attacked Rome. It was the worst siege in its history. People were shocked and terrified. Rome had been called the Eternal City and they never thought it could fall. Some Romans who were not Christian thought that the siege was a result of this "new religion." "When we had our gods, no one could even think of coming against us. The Christians' God is weak and cannot protect us," they said.

ALARIC DESCENDING ON ROME

Alaric I, the Visigoth king who attacked Rome in 410 A.D.

Augustine knew that it was important to give an answer to those accusations, and started to write. It was a very long answer—a twenty-two-volume book, written in the space of thirteen years, entitled *The City of God.* In this book, Augustine explained that there are two spiritual cities: the City of Man, made up of all those who do not love God, and the City of God, made up of those who love Him. Those two cities have been fighting from the beginning, and God has promised that the City of God will win in the end. It was important to explain that the City of God is not a kingdom of this world. After Christ came on earth, God never promised to bless a particular earthly nation, but only His spiritual kingdom composed of all believers, wherever they are. Many consider this book Augustine's masterpiece.

Many of Augustine's books were about people who, like the Manichees, called themselves Christian but taught things that were not in the Bible. Augustine knew that these wrong teachings are very dangerous. One person who was teaching errors at that time was an English monk named Pelagius, who lived for many years in Rome and then moved to Africa. Pelagius did not like what Augustine had to say, especially a prayer that Augustine had written, "Give what Thou commandest." Augustine knew he needed grace to follow God's commands.

Augustine writes *The City of God.*

Painting by Emanuele Taglietti, Ferrara, Italy

Pelagius said that God has already given us the ability to do the right things, and if we do them, we will go to heaven. He claimed that Adam and Eve just left us a bad example, but we do not have to follow it.

"No," said Augustine. "We are saved only by God's grace, which is a gift that we do not deserve. When Adam sinned, he died spiritually, and since then everyone is born spiritually dead. A dead person cannot do anything. Only God's grace can bring us to life in Jesus Christ and give us the ability to follow His rules." Augustine taught that even our love for God is a gift that God Himself puts in our hearts and helps us to obey Him with joy, not because we have to.

Vandals plundering a city

CHAPTER SEVEN
Augustine's Last Days

As Augustine became older, he realized that he had to find someone to take his place, so he chose Heraclius, the youngest of his deacons. Soon after this decision, Heraclius began preaching while Augustine sat behind him on the bishop's throne. Next to that great man of God, Heraclius felt very small, and said, "The cricket (Heraclius) chirps and the swan (Augustine) is silent."

Soon, a Northern tribe, the Vandals, came from Spain to attack the part of Africa where Augustine lived. They arrived with ships and attacked every city, robbing, killing, and burning down buildings.

They killed everyone who did not give them what they wanted, even if that person really did not have it. Augustine saw all this happening and was in tears. To the bishops who asked him if they could escape when their enemies were at their heels, he said that they should never leave behind other Christians who depended on them.

Hippo was a strong city, with high walls, and many people took refuge there. Finally, the Vandals surrounded it for many months, making sure that no one could go in and out to provide food for those inside. Every Sunday, Augustine preached to a crowd of hungry, frightened people, who felt weak in body and in their faith. He told them that God would preserve their faith until the end. Finally, he prayed that God would deliver the city, that He would give His servants the strength to face that calamity, or else that He would take him out of this world. Three months after the beginning of this siege, Augustine developed a high fever and understood that God was answering his prayer by taking him to Himself.

As he lay on his deathbed, he asked his friends to copy four psalms of David on some paper and to hang them on the walls where he could see them. They were all about repenting and asking God for forgiveness. He also asked that no one would come and see him, except during meals or during the doctor's visits, so that he could spend more time in prayer. He finally died on August 28, 430 A.D.

AUGUSTINE OF HIPPO

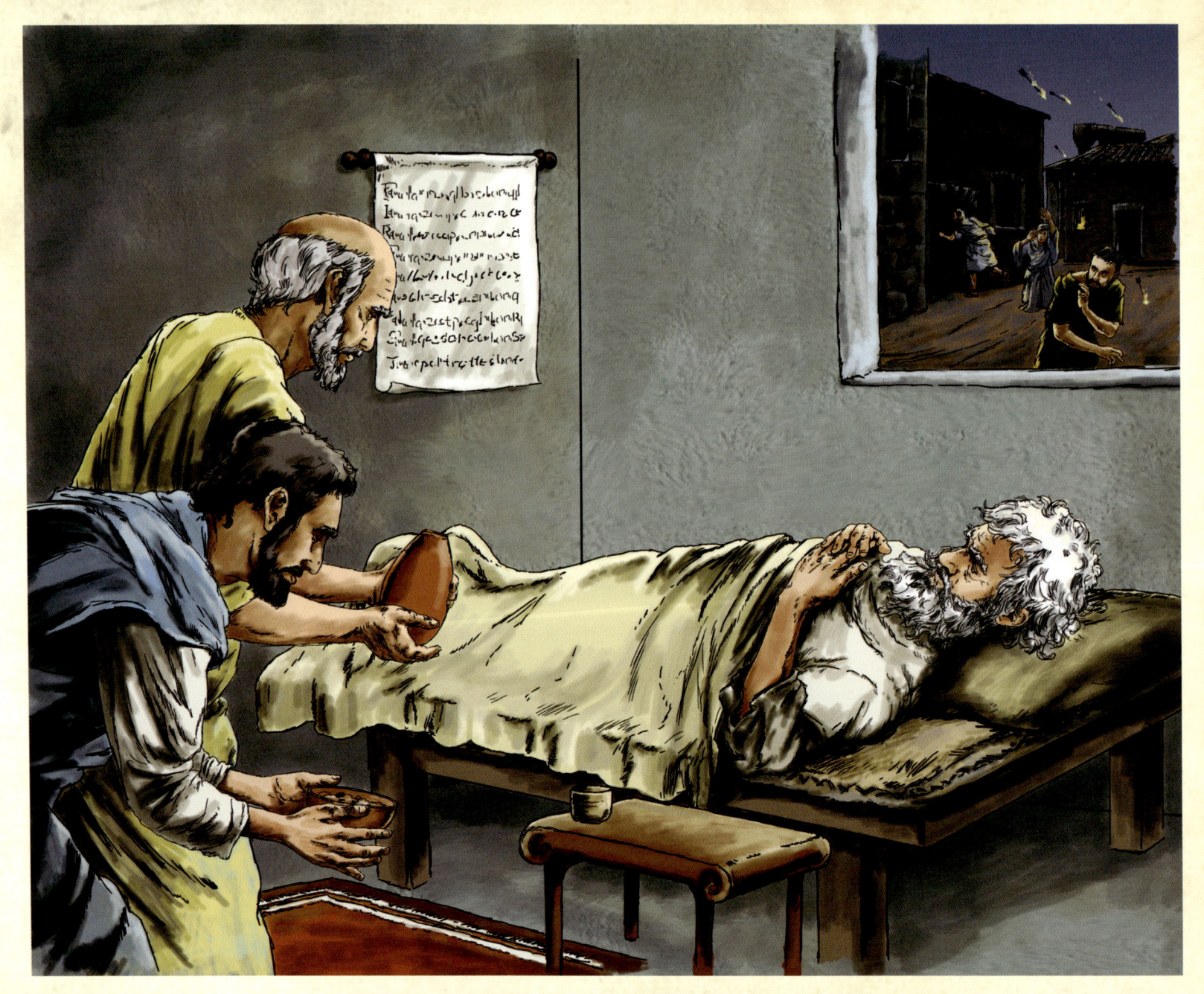

Augustine dying as Vandals attack the city of Hippo

54

About eleven months after Augustine's death, the Vandals took over Hippo and destroyed it. Some time later, those who cleared the city found that Augustine's library, full of his books, letters, and sermons, had not been burned. Augustine's writings have inspired many people after him. Many of our ideas about faith, grace, love, and our communication with our soul or with God are clear in our mind because of Augustine's explanations that have been passed on throughout the centuries.

Time Line of Augustine's Life

354 — Augustine was born in Thagaste (now in Algeria).

371 — Augustine goes to Carthage (now in Tunisia) to study.

375 — He returns to Thagaste to teach.

376 — His best friend dies. Augustine returns to Carthage.

383 — Augustine leaves for Rome.

384 — He becomes professor in Milan.

385 — Monica, his mother, meets him in Milan.

386 — He is converted and moves to a villa in Cassiciacum, near Milan.

387 — He is baptized. He leaves to go to Africa but stops in Ostia, near Rome. His mother dies.

388 — He returns to Thagaste.

391 — He is made priest in Hippo (now in Algeria).

392 — He wins a debate with Fortunatus.

395 — He is made successor of Bishop Valerius.

396 — Valerius dies.

410 — The Visigoths attack Rome. Augustine starts to write *The City of God*.

426 — Augustine appoints Heraclius as his successor.

427 — The Vandals come from Spain and invade North Africa.

430 — The Vandals besiege Hippo. Augustine dies.

Did you know?

❧ If you lived in the ancient Roman world, you could tell if people were rich or poor, slave or free, married or single just by looking at their clothes. For many centuries, the public dress for Roman men was the toga, a long piece of cloth wrapped around a tunic (or long T-shirt). In Augustine's day, fashion changed, and many rich and important men started to wear very fancy tunics with bright stockings and colorful robes. Often, there were pictures on the cloaks—sometimes flying dragons, and sometimes (for Christians) scenes from the Bible.

❧ After his conversion, Augustine chose to wear simple clothes, not too rich and not too poor, because he thought that either one of those extremes would bring attention to the person wearing them and not to Christ. He often wore a short black cloak with a hood. He never tried, however, to tell Christians how they should dress. When his follower Possidius wanted to tell believers not to wear earrings, Augustine stopped him.

❧ In most ancient paintings, we see Augustine, Ambrose, Valerius, and other Christians wearing a beard. If you look at statues of earlier Roman emperors, however, you will see that they are all shaven. Most men copied their emperors. Only philosophers and soldiers were not expected to shave. Razors were made of iron and were not as sharp as our razors today, so shaving was a painful occasion. When Emperor Hadrian, at the beginning of the second century A.D., grew a beard to conceal a scar, most Roman men were happy, because that meant that they could also avoid that painful procedure. Some emperors after him chose to shave again, setting a fashion that many people chose to follow.

- Ambrose set many Psalms to music, following Eastern melodies. Right before Augustine became a Christian, in 386, the forces of Empress Justina attacked his church building, wanting to use it for a different religion. Ambrose refused and barricaded himself inside with his congregation. The Empress ordered her forces to surround them, thinking that they would starve to death. The congregation started to sing Psalms, which encouraged them to stand strong in their faith. Some say that the soldiers outside started to sing along with the believers. Soon the siege stopped and Ambrose and his church were allowed to worship unmolested.

- In the earlier years of Roman history, people normally wrote on wax tablets using a sharp object called a *stylus*, similar to a pen without ink. Books, however, were usually written on papyrus, which was a thick material produced from the pith of the papyrus plant. Many sheets of papyrus were joined together in a scroll, usually very long (30 feet or more). In Augustine's time, a thin material called parchment, made from the skin of calves, sheep, or goats, had replaced papyrus, and pages were normally bound together in books similar to those we have today.

- In Cassiciacum, Augustine wrote some textbooks on scholastic subjects, such as grammar and some sciences. The only one of those books that is still here today is a book on musical meter, or rhythm, called *De Musica*.

- In Augustine's day, many rich Romans owned a villa, either for daily living or as a vacation home. These villas were very fancy, with frescos on the walls and mosaics on the floors. Today, we can still see some of these mosaics, which teach us how the owners of those villas spent their time—usually hunting, reading, or playing games. Often, villas had running water and even an under-floor central heating. Next to the owner's living quarters, there was often another building for the workers, the slaves, and the farm animals, and a third building where the produce from the owner's fields was stored. One could tell if a person was rich or poor by the size of his home. Around the end of the first century B.C., so many people chose to live in the cities that it became necessary to build apartments, usually 6–8 apartment blocks, three stories high or more, around an open courtyard. Maybe Augustine lived in an apartment while he taught in Rome.

- Augustine enjoyed and encouraged good conversation during meals, but he hated gossip so much that he wrote these verses on the table:

    Whoever thinks that he is able
    To nibble at the life of absent friends
    Must know that he's unworthy of this table.

    Once, when his friends forgot the rule and started to talk about someone else, he got so angry that he threatened to leave and go back to his room.

- While Augustine was bishop at Hippo, the governor of that area, Count Boniface, became a Christian. After the death of his wife, he wanted to join Augustine and his friends, but Augustine visited him and told him that he was more useful to God where he was, defending the region from enemies. Later, however, Count Boniface felt threatened by the Emperor's mother and called the Vandals for help. It was a very bad move, and Augustine tried to convince him not to do it. When Count Boniface found out that the person threatening him was not the Emperor's mother, and that all was well with Rome, he tried to send the Vandals back but it was too late. Finally, he had to run for his life, finding temporary refuge in Hippo.

❧ As the Vandals continued to destroy North Africa, one exiled bishop took the body of Augustine with him to the island of Sardinia. However, Sardinia was not safe either. Some time later, a king of the Lombards moved Augustine's body again, this time to Pavia, Italy, where it is kept today inside the Cathedral of St. Peter in Ciel d'Oro.